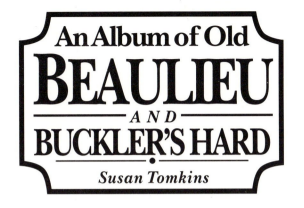

An Album of Old
BEAULIEU
A N D
BUCKLER'S HARD

Susan Tomkins

Ensign
PUBLICATIONS

Published in 1990 by
Ensign Publications
A division of Hampshire Books Ltd
2 Redcar Street
Southampton SO1 5LL

Typeset & designed by PageMerger, Southampton

Edited by Susan Tomkins and David Graves

Jacket front: Beaulieu Village *c.*,1906. William Winsey, proprietor stands outside his grocery shop. There has long been a store on this site – from the mid 18th to the mid 19th century the Westbrook family ran a large general store from these premises – and today the shop still sells general provisions.

Jacket back: Guns and beaters setting out for a shoot from Bergerie Farm in 1910. (See also page 58).

British Library Cataloguing in Publication Data
Tomkins, Susan
  An album of old Beaulieu and Bucklers Hard.
  1. Hampshire. Beaulieu, history
  I. Title
  942.2'75

ISBN 1 85455 046 2

INTRODUCTION

Nearly eight-hundred years ago the Cistercian Abbey of Beaulieu was founded by King John. He gave the monks an estate of over 10,000 acres in the New Forest on which to build their abbey and support their community. This they did for three hundred and fifty years until the abbey was closed by Henry VIII in 1538 as part of the Dissolution of the Monasteries. He sold the land (and the buildings that survived his demolition orders) to Sir Thomas Wriothesley for £1,340-6s-8d – the Beaulieu Estate had the first of its fourteen Lords of the Manor.

Links with the original monastic land grant still remain and are very much in evidence. Three of the abbey buildings have been converted to serve new functions. Shortly after Dissolution, the Choir Monks' Refectory became the Parish Church of Beaulieu. The Great Gatehouse where the abbot received his guests was turned into the Wriothesley hunting lodge called Palace House. The Domus, once home to the lay brothers, has had a variety of uses over the years – parson's house, brewery, agricultural store and concert hall, to name but a few.

Beaulieu village probably began life as a series of fairly mean hovels and temporary dwellings belonging to the people who came to the abbey to provide the monks with crafts and trades they were unable to supply from within their own ranks. Later, as the dwellings became more permanent, their numbers would have been increased by people seeking sanctuary from a variety of crimes ranging from debt to murder. If the King's men were to arrive the miscreants could take shelter inside the abbey walls until the danger had passed. In the years, following Dissolution the village acquired a mill, grocers, drapers, blacksmiths, saddlers, wheelwrights and several public houses. A workhouse for the estate poor opened in 1794 on the site of the old almshouses and separate schools for boys, girls and infants were provided in the mid-19th century. The village had its own horse and cattle fair but this was closed shortly before the turn of the century because of drunken behaviour and the scuffles which broke out between the men of Beaulieu and East Boldre.

Most of the abbey's granges and specialist production centres have continued to be worked as farming units down to the present day, although the balance between arable and pasture has fluctuated in accordance with national and international policies. In fact, the area under cultivation is larger than that in monastic times because of the reclamation work carried out by farmers in the 17th and 18th centuries. The units still retain their grange names; Hartford, Sowley, St Leonard's and Otterwood. Bouverie, the centre for cattle is now Beufre Farm; Bergerie Farm was the sheep and wool store.

Warren Farm the site of the monks' vast rabbit warrens; and Gins Farm, named after a piece of lifting equipment, was where the monks kept the boats which formed their fishing fleet. Other areas of the original monastic estate survive topographically; Salternshill, where the monks may have evaporated salt from the waters of the Beaulieu River; Abbotstanding, part of the abbot's hunting ground; and Monkeyshorn Farm, "Monk's Corner", standing in an angle of the monastic boundary.

The Beaulieu Abbey Charter conveyed not only land to the monks, but more unusually, it gave them rights of ownership over the bed and foreshore of the Beaulieu River, together with rights of wreck, flotsam and jetsam. These rights have been inherited by the Lord of the Manor, and tested in his favour as recently as 1927.

There have of course been developments over the years which have more tenuous links with the monastic origins of the Estate. The early 18th century saw the clearing of Dungehill Copse on the edge of the Beaulieu River. This was initiated by John, 2nd Duke of Montagu as a site for his planned freeport, Montagu Town, which would import and export sugar from the West Indian islands of St. Lucia and St. Vincent. Sadly the plan failed but some forty years later the village, now called Buckler's Hard, became a centre for the building of wooden ships for George III's navy. It thrived until the advent of iron ships in the 19th century when it became a sleepy rural retreat. Naval shipbuilding returned during the First and Second World Wars, but today it is the yachting facilities which bring boats to Buckler's Hard.

Large-scale tourism is one of the most significant developments on the estate in recent years. Its scale and nature would surprise a time-travelling Beaulieu monk, but as an idea it would not be unfamiliar – the medieval equivalent was the pilgrimage to foreign and domestic shrines. The first Beaulieu tourists came in the 18th century to visit the picturesque abbey ruins. They came more formally at the turn of the century when Lord Montagu's grandfather allowed ferry passengers to disembark at Buckler's Hard, and following excavation work on the ruins, an abbey museum was opened and cream teas were served in the domus. Palace House first welcomed visitors in 1952 and the National Motor Museum followed some twenty years later. Today's visitors to the Museum, House and Abbey help to contribute to the costs of maintaining, conserving and restoring the historic buildings on the estate.

The photographs and drawings in this book reflect both remarkable continuity and some change on the Beaulieu Estate over the years. Some places have altered beyond recognition, others have undergone minor modifications over the years, whilst some are little changed from the days of the monks. To recognise the category into which each picture falls is one of the pleasures of leafing through this delightful picture book.

The Beaulieu Band marching past the Montagu Arms. The brass band was a prominent feature of village life from the late 19th century until just after the First World War, playing at concerts and teas, and at the head of processions to the Church. Led by Tom Gregory playing his silver cornet, the band was much in evidence at Queen Victoria's Diamond Jubilee Celebrations in 1897, and in concerts for the organ fund and to raise money to renew its own instruments.

6

Beaulieu Village School Group, *c.,*1890.

Beaulieu Post Office, pre-1921. From the turn of the century until 1921 the Post Office was located in Warner's House, which takes its name from the estate steward, William Warner who, with his son, held the tenancy from 1735 to 1811. From the 1830's to the 1860's, it was home to the Misses Adams, descendants of the Master Builder, Henry Adams. For much of this century it has been occupied by the Misses Burden whose family were the village millers.

Beaulieu Village Street at the turn of the century. The gabled roof of Palace House can be seen between the trees in the centre left of the picture.

Buccleuch Cottages, 1863. The cottages named after their builder, the 5th Duke of Buccleuch, were built in 1863, mainly to provide houses for the schoolmaster, James Stevens, and the schoolmistress, Miss Prophett. The former occupied the house in the foreground, and Miss Prophett the adjoining one. A little later a parish nurse was provided, largely at the expense of the estate and she occupied another of the houses.

The Montagu Arms, pre-1887. This photograph shows the 18th century building, but there had been an inn on the site since the 16th century, known as the 'Ship', then the 'George' and since 1742, 'The Montagu Arms'. The stable-yard is out of the picture on the left. The Inn consisted of a tap room, a bar and a meeting room. This front was demolished in 1887.

11

The Montagu Arms, *c.,*1900. This photograph, issued as a postcard by the proprietor of the inn, shows the alterations of 1887. The east wing, at this time consisting of stables, was not completed until 1926.

Meeting of the Otter Hunt outside the Montagu Arms, 1909. The new front can clearly be seen in this photograph, but not until 1925 was the north-east wing added. The Inn was the meeting place for farmers and parish officers and a centre for timber auctions and lectures as well as providing food and accommodation. There was even a cattle market held here until the 1890's and the Inn had its own farmland. (P. Mansell)

Beaulieu Village Street *c.,*1900. In the centre right of the photograph are Morris' House and Warner's House. These were built in the early eighteenth century on the site of a hop garden. Morris' House is named after Alexander Morris, who ran a building business, and was responsible for much of the brickbuilding on the Estate, including the first houses at Montagu Town (Buckler's Hard).

Loading Grain at Beaulieu Tide Mill, *c.,*1852. It is possible that this photograph was taken during the village's celebrations for the coming-of-age of the future 6th Duke of Buccleuch. On the left are the old mangold house, the mill flume, now-demolished cottages, the mill sluices and the archway of the Gatehouse, through which can be seen a marquee on the Palace House lawns. To the right is the entrance to the Mill buildings and the Mill House beyond.

Loading Grain at Beaulieu Tide Mill, *c.,*1900. The first mill recorded on this site, just over the bridge from the Outer Gatehouse, appears in 1576 and since then has remained in this position, although it has not worked as a mill for over forty years. The miller was one of the leading men in the parish. His monopoly meant all tenants were required to bring their grain to him and be charged a toll for the service. The principal milling families in Beaulieu were the Barneys (1740-1849), the Burdens (1862-1922) and the Norris' (1876-1922).

16

The Dairy in the Garden of Beaulieu Mill. The Dairy was put to an unusual use by Sappers and the Home Guard of Beaulieu during the Second World War – it was a camouflaged strong point to protect the village from German invasion. Anti-tank defences were built onto the Gatehouse together with a gun emplacement, and further strong points were built in the old mangold house and several cow sheds.

The Pool, Beaulieu, *c.,*1920, located at the back of the Mill Buildings and fed by the Beaulieu River.

Beaulieu Village Street, 1914. The 'G.N.' Cycle Car is parked outside Beaulieu Manor Office from where the business of the estate was conducted. The agent at this time was Mr. Gerard Morgan, assisted by J.W. Nash-Brown, but Morgan was soon to be replaced by Capt. H.E.R. Widnell, estate steward, archivist and historian for over sixty years.

Brummidges & Widow Russel's House, *c.,1863.* The timber-framed house was the 'Crown Inn' in 1694 but by 1715 it had become known as 'Brummidges', the home of Francis Bromwich, Minister of Beaulieu. On the right is the brickbuilt house of a Widow Russel and originally they formed two detached homes on this site. By 1845 each had been divided into two and a small building inserted between them to make the row of five tenements seen in the photograph.

The Boy's School, Beaulieu, 1863. Built by the 5th Duke of Buccleuch to provide extra space for the boys, girls and infants schools in the village. Until the Education Act of 1870, educational opportunities were provided by the Montagu and Buccleuch families as part of their charity work. It is believed that this photograph may have been taken on the school's opening day and that the man in the top hat is the schoolmaster, Mr. James Stevens.

The 4th Volunteer Battalion Hants Cyclists, Beaulieu, 1907. The Estate often provided sites for camps because the authorities were reluctant to allow the use of Forest land. They usually camped in the fields just inside the abbey walls and their presence was good for local tradesmen. It is interesting to note that the card is postmarked 'Beaulieu Camp'.

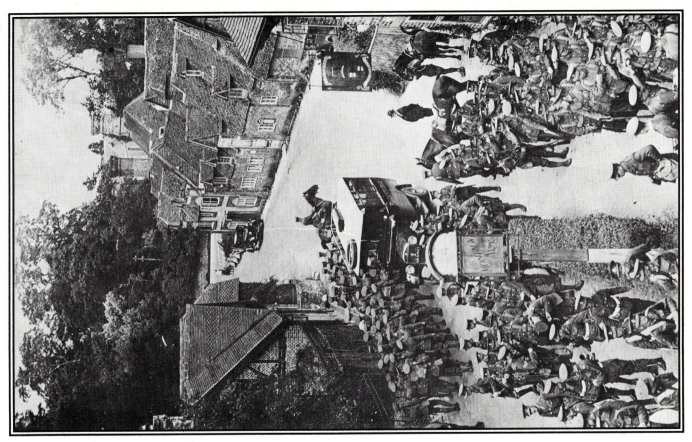

The 5th Royal West Kents (Territorials) outside the Montagu Arms, August 1930. The Division were en route to their camp at Hatchett Pond. Beaulieu Mill Buildings can be seen in the background and just behind is the Church. (P. Mansell)

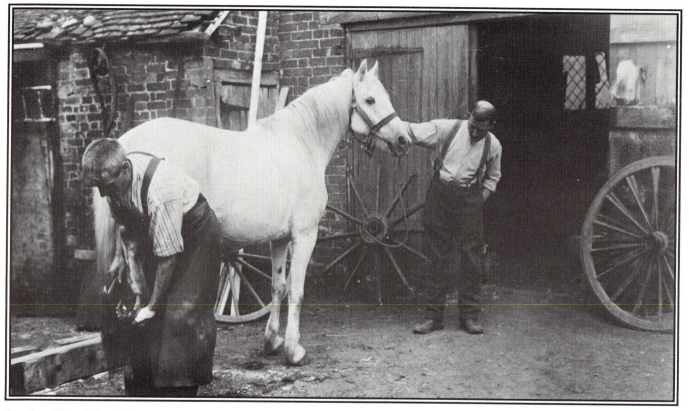

Blacksmith at Work, 20th century. Beaulieu village had several smithies. This one was on the west side of the street on a site which had previously housed the infant school. The Payne family ran both the smithy and a wheelwright's workshop, and it continued as a blacksmith's until 1960.

Beaulieu Cricket Pavilion, *c.,*1900. Situated to the east of Beaulieu Abbey, the pitch was laid on the orders of Henry, Lord Montagu (seen 6th from right) who wished to encourage his employees in healthy pursuits. Matches were played against neighbouring estates and although Henry did not play, Beaulieu benefitted from the presence of his son-in-law, the Hampshire gentleman cricketer, Harry Forster. The season usually ended with a "married versus single" match.

A Postcard showing the teams for a match between the ladies of Beaulieu and the men of Beaulieu Cricket Club. The first match was at the end of the 1912 season, with the ladies fielding 18 players to the mens 11. The men had to field, bat and bowl left-handed, but still managed to restrict the ladies to 72 runs. They replied with 131 runs, Miss Self from the Montagu Arms taking all the wickets apart from two run-outs.

The Teams for the return match in July 1913 which the ladies, fielding 22 players to the mens 11, managed to win. They scored 222 runs, the men 151.

Beaulieu Royal Mail Postal Van, *c.,*1920-21. James Biddlecombe had been the village miller, but on retirement took over the driving of the evening mail van to Brockenhurst Station. His faithful horse was a war veteran; eventually they both retired from the journey in the 1930's to be replaced by motorized transport.

Beaulieu Fire Brigade, 1908. Lord & Lady Montagu and daughter, Helen, seen with the Beaulieu Volunteer Fire Brigade. The manual fire engine was driven by Mr. Jones, the village carrier with his own horse or with horses from the Montagu Arms or Mr. Winsey, the grocer. Some of the Brigade were Estate workers like Frank Wadley, engineer at the Beaulieu Electric Light Station (standing, second from left) and Alexander "Harry" Pattillo, plumber (second row, first left). Others worked in the village like Harry Wells from the Garage & Bicycle Works (back row, second from right).

Palace House Gardeners, *c.,*1909. The Head Gardener, Mr. Lee, can be seen wearing the straw hat at the front of the picture – with his nine under-gardeners and journeymen he was responsible for providing Palace House with fruit, vegetables and flowers all year round. Out of season varieties could, with care and attention, be produced in the glasshouse on the left.

Mowing the Palace House Lawns, *c.,***1900.** In the days before motorised lawnmowers horses were harnessed to the machines to provide extra power. Note the special horse shoes worn to protect the lawns from hoof damage.

Foresters at Work in Hartford Wood, early 20th century. Timber formed and indeed still does form, an important part of the Estate economy. Until 1867 it was sold by auction at the Montagu Arms, since then it has been sold by private treaty. At the time of the photograph profits on woodland products varied between £780 and £1000 a year. Wood was sold to coal-mine owners for pit props, to charcoal burners and to makers of gateposts and fences. Coopers bought it for barrels and bavins were used in the Estate brickworks.

Plough Teams at Beaulieu, 20th century. On the right of the photograph is David Kitcher, clerk of works and head forester of the Beaulieu Estate for many years. Although seen with plough in hand, this was a time when the amount of wheat and barley grown on the Estate was falling due to increasing overseas competition. The Estate's farmers were changing over to dairying. The two greys being handled here by ploughman Charlie were Captain and Jewel.

Gathering the Harvest on the Beaulieu Estate, early 20th century.

The Kitchen, Palace House, *c.,***1905-6.** The cook, Annie Louise Freeman (seen on left) at work with her kitchenmaids. The opened door in the background leads to the scullery, which until recently housed the family and estate records.

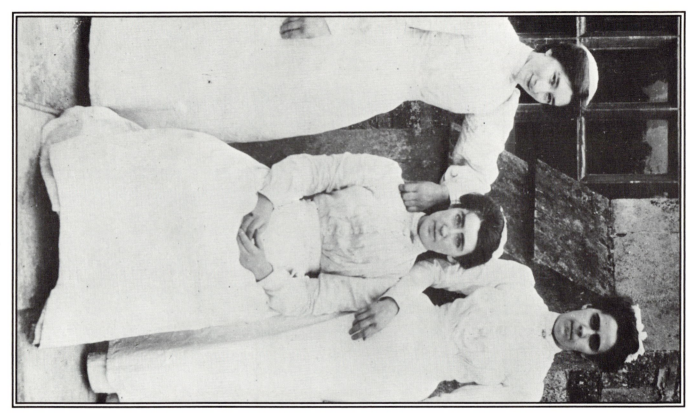

Annie Louise Freeman with her kitchen staff, *c.,*1905. Taken outside the back door of Palace House.

Aerial View of Beaulieu Abbey Ruins, *c.,*1960's. Two of the surviving abbey buildings can be seen; the Domus in the centre and to the left the refectory (now the Parish Church) together with two walls of the Cloisters. On the right are the outlines of the abbey Church, knocked flat on the orders of Henry VIII to prevent the monks from re-establishing the abbey. In the background is the Montagu Motor Museum and the kitchen/market garden supplying Palace House.

Restoration of Domus Interior, 1909. The Domus Conversorum was one of the few monastic buildings to survive the abbey's dissolution in 1538. Over the years it has served many purposes; dining hall and dormitory for the monastic lay brothers, parson's house, brewery, and agricultural store. Since its restoration the upper floor seen here, has been used for Estate concerts, entertainments and dinners, and the lower floor as a museum and exhibition of monastic life.

Beaulieu Church, published 1800. An engraving by W. Byrne from a drawing by T. Hearne of the old Choir Monks Refectory at Beaulieu Abbey. Some fifty years or so after dissolution it became the Parish Church of Beaulieu. The pulpit, still used by the vicar, was where a monk would stand to read aloud from the Bible whilst the meal was in progress.

One of the first dances held in the restored Domus. The edge of the Minstrel's Gallery can be seen top left.

The Outer Gatehouse, Palace House, pre-1885. The building dates from the 14th century and it was from here that the porter of Beaulieu Abbey used to dispense alms in the form of food and clothing to the poor. The clock is of course a much later adornment. Its working occupied the small chamber above the porch and the rods which worked the hands protruded through two Early English lancet lights. In 1885, Henry, Lord Montagu had the clock moved to the turret above, and the Gatehouse became a home for Estate workers.

Palace House across the Beaulieu River, early 20th century. The clock added to the turret of the Gatehouse in 1885 can clearly be seen, as can the gables of Palace House. These were added in the early 18th century together with turrets, a moat, and a drawbridge by John, 2nd Duke of Montagu. He wanted to fortify his manor house against possible invasion by the French. The moat was never filled because of its above sea-level site.

The Old Entrance Porch, Palace House, pre-1870's. A country house party captured on camera shortly after the marriage of Lord Henry Scott (fourth from left at back) to Lady Cecily Stuart-Wortley (fourth from right up steps) in 1865. The couple were given the Beaulieu Estate as a wedding present by Henry's father, the Duke of Buccleuch.

Palace House, c.,1900. Henry, Lord Montagu, his wife, Lady Cecily and their family relaxing in the grounds of their home. The monastic Great Gatehouse with its arched windows can be seen on the left of the picture. At right angles to this is the East Wing added in the 1870's, whilst on the extreme left is the billiard room added at the same time. The formal flower borders in the foreground are a typical design for this period.

The Upper Drawing Room, Palace House, early 20th century. This room formed one of two chapels above the porches of the monastic Great Gatehouse. On the right of the photograph, the piscina and aumbry can be seen marking the line of the altar across the room with the draught screens. The aumbry was used for storing vessels used in the mass, the piscina for rinsing the communion plate and chalice after a service.

The Lower Drawing Room, Palace House, pre-1870's. The small fireplace in the left foreground of the picture was replaced during the alterations of the 1870's by a huge imitation medieval, hooded fireplace. Its installation reflected both the monastic origins of the building and the current fashion for a Gothic revival. Early teething problems, resulting in more smoke filling the room than disappearing up the chimney, were eventually solved.

The Lower Drawing Room, Palace House, pre-1870's. Originally the first entrance porch to the 14th century Great Gatehouse of Beaulieu Abbey where the abbot received his guests. The large archways on the right of the photograph would have been open to provide pedestrian and carriage access. After the abbey was dissolved, the gatehouse was converted into a hunting lodge and then a manor house with this room serving as an entrance hall until the alterations of the 1870's when it became a drawing room.

Restoration Work, Palace House, 1978-9. Maintenance and conservation work on historic properties is an on-going task. Here a Palace House chimney is being cleaned and repaired. Similar work was also carried out on the roof, moat turrets, and gargoyles. Beaulieu Parish Church can be seen in the background.

Beaulieu Celebrations for Queen Victoria's Golden Jubilee, 22nd June, 1887. Held in the grounds to the north of Beaulieu Abbey, the festivities included athletic sports like hurdle races, a tug-of-war and a 'greasy pole', musical entertainment from the Beaulieu Band and a speech by Henry, Lord Montagu. Tea was served in marquees erected in the ruined "Wine-Press" building (centre of photograph) and queues were reported to be long and slow-moving – hardly surprising as *c.*,1400 people are said to have attended! At the end of the day Henry distributed Jubilee medals.

Salterns Hill Farm, 1905. There has been a farm on this site since the beginning of the 16th century when the monks of Beaulieu leased it to Alice Naylor. Its name suggests that the area, close to the Beaulieu River, had previously been used as a saltern, a place where sea-water is evaporated to form salt. One of the later tenants of the farm was Edward Adams, son of Henry Adams, the Master Builder, and part-owner of the Buckler's Hard Shipyard.

Draining Sowley Pond, 1907. Sowley Pond was constructed by the Beaulieu Abbey monks in 1270. They built a causeway to prevent the waters of two streams reaching the sea, and in doing so flooded a lime kiln in a local settlement, much to the annoyance of its inhabitants. The pond supplied the abbey with fish and at the end of the 19th century the pond was once more providing fish for the dinner table. Charles Braun had established a trout fishery, but by 1907 was facing problems caused by pike in the pond eating the trout. The pond was drained to remove the pike, which as the picture shows, proved of great local interest.

Interior of St. Leonard's Barn, *c.,*1900. The barn, built by the monks of Beaulieu Abbey in the 13th century was one of the largest monastic barns in the country with a capacity of ½ million cubic feet. St. Leonard's was once one of the granges supplying produce to the abbey. Its principal crop was grain, in the form of oats and wheat. The barn was used as a store and in winter for threshing grain on a special section of the floor. In the 16th century parts of it were knocked down and the material used to build a smaller barn inside the shell of the old one, seen here on the left of the picture. Both shell and barn remain in use.

The Royal Oak Public House, Hill Top, *c.*,1900. Today the 'Royal Oak' still stands at the north-eastern corner of the monastic estate. Here, a delivery from the wine merchants is being received whilst the horses take advantage of the break to feed from their nose bags.

Work on the Beaulieu Oyster Beds, late 19th century. These beds were located between Buckler's Hard and Gins Farm on the Beaulieu River. There had always been small oyster beds near Need's Ore which were rented out, but in 1869, Henry, Lord Montagu took over management of the River and built these further upstream. He founded the Newtown Oyster Company and sought advice from marine biologists and French breeders. In the 1880's, Beaulieu oysters were considered a great delicacy but they were extremely expensive to produce and by 1906 the beds were closed. The beds were re-used during the Second World War to help build a concrete floating dock and parts of the Mulberry Harbours.

Opening of the Golf Club House at Warren Beach. John and Cecil, 2nd Lord & Lady Montagu can be seen seated in deckchairs in the centre of the photograph, Cecil wearing a veiled motoring hat. The Club House was build *c.*,1912-13 on Gravelley Marsh, Warren Shore. In 1947 the Hon. Ewen Montagu QC took a lease on the 'Old Club House Bungalow' and lived there until his death in 1985.

Return of John & Cecil, 2nd Lord & Lady Montagu of Beaulieu, 6th July, 1889. The Hon. John Scott-Montagu married his cousin, Lady Cecil Kerr, daughter of the 9th Marquess of Lothian at St. George's, Hanover Square on the 4th June, 1889. It was one of the most fashionable weddings of the year, attended by the Prime Minister, Lord Salisbury. They honeymooned at Blickling Hall, Norfolk, and returned to Beaulieu on the 6th July to take up residence at the Lodge, the old vicarage in the village now home to Lord Montagu's mother, Mrs. Pleydell-Bouverie. The couple are seen about to pass through the outer gatehouse into the grounds of Palace House for a celebratory garden party.

Shooting Party in Hartford Wood, early 20th century. This is said to be the last stag shot on the Beaulieu Estate. John, 2nd Lord Montagu is on the left.

Guns & Beaters ready for the Shoot at Bergerie Farm, 1910. The guns from left to right are: Comte Clery, Mr. Noble, John, Lord Montagu, his brother-in-law Harry Forster of Lepe, and his cousin Archibald Stuart-Wortley, Thomas Sharp, Gaston Duplessis, Marquis of Headfort, Sir James Fowler (Beaulieu Abbey historian) and Sir Thomas Troubridge (Abbey Custodian), and Jack Forster, John's nephew. The harbourmaster, Mr. Thomas can be seen through the glass of the car.

The Motorcycle Museum, Palace House, 1955. The exhibits were housed in the kitchen and courtyard of Palace House, and together with the cars gave the house a very oily smell!

Exterior of the Montagu Motor Museum, 1956. By this time Lord Montagu's collection of cars and motorcycles had outgrown the available space in Palace House. These wooden buildings were constructed to the north of the house to display the vehicles and were formally opened by Lord Brabazon of Tara and Geoff Duke, the reigning World Motorcycling Champion.

Interior of the Montagu Motor Museum, pre-1959. Here the 16-cylinder B.R.M. racing car can be seen on the right, but once again this collection of exhibits was growing too fast for its accommodation so in 1959 a new Montagu Motor Museum was opened adjacent to the old one by Lord Brabazon of Tara.

Transferring Exhibits from the Montagu Motor Museum to the National Motor Museum , 20th June, 1972. The Museum's entire collection was moved overnight from the old building to the new to maintain its record of being open every day. Some cars were driven to their new home, others like this one needed a tow! The fountain had to be dismantled and its pond planked over to provide easy access between the two museums.

The Opening of the National Motor Museum by HRH the Duke of Kent, 4th July, 1972. In front of the Duke as he makes his speech is a miniature Sunbeam 'Club' car presented to him by Lord Montagu's children, Ralph and Mary.

Beaulieu and the Beaulieu River, taken by Commander Penrose, 1945. In the centre of the picture is the Millpond, built to power Beaulieu Mill. To its left over the bridge is Palace House and the road to Hill Top. To its right are the buildings of Beaulieu Village. In the distance is the Isle of Wight.

Palace House and Grounds, *c.,***1970.** One of the main features of interest in this aerial view of the Beaulieu complex is the building site to the top left. This is early construction work on the National Motor Museum and Brabazon Catering Suite. To its right are the ruins of an abbey building, known for many years as the Wine-Press. Recent excavation work has suggested it may have been a medieval fulling mill.

Bath Cottage, *c.*,1900. Built in 1760 by the Duke of Montagu for his arthritic son, the Marquess of Monthermer, who was advised to try salt-water baths in the Beaulieu River as a form of treatment. Over the years the cottage has served as home to labourers' families, a holiday retreat, and a yachtsman's clubhouse.

The Gosport Ferry, c.,1900. In 1894 the Gosport Steam Launch Company began running day excursions to Buckler's Hard on Saturdays, bank holidays and mid-week. Sunday trips were prohibited until 1906. In 1896 these visitors would have paid 1s 8d each for the return trip from Gosport to Buckler's Hard, a price which included a pier toll of 2d per adult and 1d per child. In the first six months of the operation, 1,115 adults and 84 children landed at Buckler's Hard.

Building the Experimental Concrete Dry Dock, 1943-44. The old oyster beds downstream of Buckler's Hard were used for the building of this floating dock. A hundred men were involved in the construction. Work took place amid great secrecy, although most local people knew what was happening. The dock was launched on 25th March, 1944 and has been used for the repair of destroyers in Ceylon, North Africa, and most recently in Norway – a good record for an experimental design used to combat a steel shortage.

Buckler's Hard Village, *c.*,1950. A small ship repair yard stands where 200 years previously wooden men-of-war were built for the navy of King George III. The cottage terraces which once housed shipyard workers and labourers are now home to estate staff. The motor car has begun to invade the wide main street where the huge ship timbers were left to season, and the village water pump has disappeared. The site of the saw pit in the foreground has been taken over by vegetation – and a sign of things to come, pleasure yachts moored along the River.

West Terrace, Buckler's Hard, *c.,***1966.** A few yards up the street with a good view over the berths is the Master Builder's House where Henry Adams lived. Adams was the most famous of the village's shipbuilders and even after retirement kept a strict eye on the workers from the bay window of his study, seen in the centre of this photograph. There is a story that each worker wore a numbered shirt. When Adams saw something which displeased him, he would send for the numbered miscreant. Today, Adams' home is a hotel and restaurant.

QUEEN MARY ARRIVING AT BUCKLERS HARD.

Queen Mary arriving at Buckler's Hard. The old 18th century shipbuilding berths can be seen in the right foreground. Here, ships like HMS Agamemnon, Euryalus and Swiftsure were built for Nelson's navy. These ships saw service at the Battle of Trafalgar in 1805.

THE QUEEN ARRIVING AT BUCKLERS HARD WITH LORD MONTAGU.

Queen Mary arriving at Buckler's Hard with John, 2nd Lord Montagu on her left.

Queen Mary arriving at Buckler's Hard, August 1927. The visit took place during Cowes Week. Queen Mary was picked up from the Royal Yacht, 'Victoria & Albert' by John, Lord Montagu in his motor yacht 'Cygnet' and brought to Buckler's Hard. Her equerry, Sir Harold Verney (third from left) had the job of making sure that the gangplank was safe before Her Majesty stepped ashore, to be taken to Palace House for tea in Lord Montagu's Rolls Royce Phantom.

A Group of Children at Buckler's Hard, *c.,*1920's. Many of these youngsters followed in their parents' footsteps and found employment on the Beaulieu Estate and River. Stanley Seaman, on the far right of the photograph, worked for a time in Wrann's Ship Repair Yard. He remembers as a child taking part in large-scale games played in the village street, including football, played with a ball of flaming rags.

Tea Shop, Buckler's Hard, *c.,* **1920's.** Mrs. Corbin, with her young daughter, seen at the door of her shop in the East Terrace of the village. She served cream teas and sold postcards and sweets to the 2,000 day trippers who arrived in the village each year on the Gosport Ferry. The shop was once the Ship Inn, serving shipwrights and caulkers in the 18th century. Today, it is a private residence.

West Terrace, Buckler's Hard, *c.,***1920's/30's.** At this time these houses were all homes for estate workers, with the exception of number 82 (extreme right of picture) which has served as a small chapel since 1886. It has also housed an infants' school, a cobbler's shop, and according to local lore, a smuggler's den. If true, it must have made for an interesting life as the government's Salt Officers lived in the terrace during the period when smuggling was at its height. Number 74, on the left end of the terrace, is now the village shop.

East Terrace, Buckler's Hard, early 20th century. The terrace once contained the village's two public alehouses, the Ship Inn (where the 'Teas' sign hangs in the photograph) and the New Inn at its highest end. It now forms part of the Maritime Museum, where a reconstruction of its interior, *c.,1793*, can be seen. The picture was taken by the local photographer, E.W. Mudge, whose car can be seen at the top of the street.

ENSIGN PUBLICATIONS

Ensign Publications publish a wide range of local interest books on a variety of interesting topics. Uniform with this series are the books featured opposite, they can all be obtained by writing to the address below. We will be pleased to send you an invoice including post and packing or you can purchase the books from bookshops and newsagents in the featured places.

For a complete catalogue of our books on Hampshire, Dorset, Sussex and Wiltshire write to:

Ensign Publications
Redcar Street
Southampton SO1 5LL

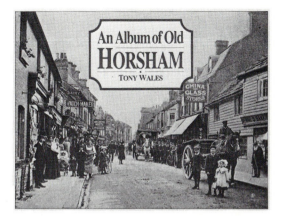

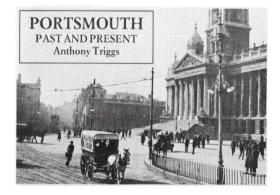

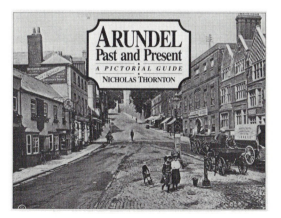

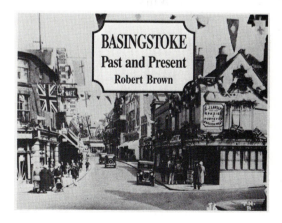